A Christian Holistic & Wholeness Devotional
Copyright © 2025 by Teya Gibson

All rights reserved. No part of this publication may be reproduced, distributed, or transmitted in any form or by any means, including photocopying, recording, or other electronic or mechanical methods, without the prior written permission of the author, except in the case of brief quotations embodied in critical reviews and certain other non-commercial uses permitted by copyright law.

Tellwell Talent
www.tellwell.ca

ISBN
978-1-7642959-0-1 (Paperback)

# Hello & Welcome

My heart in creating this devotional is to help people thrive fully and freely as God intended. When we surrender every part of our lives to Him, transformation begins.

Over six weeks, we'll focus on key areas of wholeness: spiritual, mental, physical, emotional, relational, and financial realigning your life with God's design, one day at a time.

This isn't just a journal. It's a space to slow down, hear God, build healthy rhythms, and walk toward lasting change. Wherever you're starting from, I'm so glad you're here. Let's take it one day at a time together.

*Teya Gibson*

SPIRITUALLY ANCHORED

FINANCIALLY
EMPOWERED

MENTALLY
CLEAR

## Elements of Christ Centered Wholeness

RELATIONALLY
CONNECTED

PHYSICALLY
STRONG

EMOTIONALLY FREE

# Table of Devotional Contents.

**Spiritual Wholeness;** *Rooted in Christ* — 07
  Week One

**Mental Wholeness;** *Renewed in Truth* — 23
  Week Two

**Physical Wholeness;** *Honouring the Body* — 39
  Week Three

**Emotional Wholeness;** *Fully Feeling, Healing Deeply* — 55
  Week Four

**Relational Wholeness;** *Cultivating Christlike Connection* — 71
  Week Five

**Financial Wholeness;** *Trusting God with Our Treasures* — 87
  Week Six

# Your Daily Rythm

*What to expect each day on your journey towards wholeness*

### A Scripture
A verse to ground your focus in God's Word.

### Devotional Thought
A short, soul-nourishing reflection to encourage, challenge, and help align your perspective with the word of God.

### Wellness Habit
A simple, practical action to embody that day's focus and bring the truth of the word of God into your everyday life.

### Reflection Prompt
Journaling questions to help you process, explore, and respond to what God is doing in you.

### Guided Prayer
A written prayer to anchor your heart and invite God into your day.

### Gratitude & Notes
A space to give thanks, jot down insights, or simply be present with your thoughts.

Week 1: Day 1
# Abide in The Vine
Spiritual Wholeness: Rooted In Christ

 *"I am the sprouting vine and you're my branches. As you live in union with me as your source, fruitfulness will stream from within you but when you live separated from me you are powerless."* John 15:5 TPT

Jesus invites us into union, not obligation. In a world that glorifies hustle and self-effort, this verse is a gentle rebuke and a glorious reminder: we are not the vine. He is. You and I were never meant to sustain ourselves, produce spiritual fruit on our own, or find our identity in our output.

The call to abide is not passive it's deeply intentional. It means choosing connection over control, presence over performance. It's a soul posture that says, *"Jesus, I trust You to be my Source."* When you live in that place of union with Him, everything else flows from it your joy, your purpose, your peace, your health.

If you've been running on empty, this is your invitation to come back to the Vine. Not to do more but to receive more. Because separation drains, but connection sustains

**DEVOTIONAL THOUGHT**

 **Wellness Habit**
Go outside today even if just for a short walk and spend 10 quiet minutes with Jesus. Ask Him: *"Where am I striving without You?"* and *"Where do You want to fill me again?"*

In what ways have you been trying to 'produce fruit' in your own strength? What does it look like for you to return to abiding in Christ today?

SPIRITUAL WHOLENESS: ROOTED IN CHRIST

7

**Prayer**

Jesus, I'm tired of striving. I've let busyness replace intimacy. Today, I come back to You my Vine, my Source. I lay down every area I've tried to control or carry alone. Teach me to remain in You, to breathe in Your peace, and to bear fruit that lasts. Abide in me as I abide in You. Amen.

## GRATITUDE & NOTES

SPIRITUAL WHOLENESS: ROOTED IN CHRIST

Week 1: Day 2
# You are God's Masterpiece
Spiritual Wholeness: Rooted In Christ

*We have become His poetry, a re-created people that will fulfill the destiny He has given each of us, for we are joined to Jesus, the Anointed One. Even before we were born, God planned in advance our destiny and the good works we would do to fulfill it!*
Ephesians 2:10 TPT

You are not a mistake. You are God's intentional, handcrafted design His poetry. The Latin word used here is *Imago Dei*, meaning *Image Bearer*. You were created for a destiny, one that reflects His goodness and glory.

The world may measure you by success, status, or performance, but God already calls you whole. When we lose sight of our identity in Him, we begin to chase validation elsewhere through people, achievements, or constant striving.

But when you know you're His masterpiece, you begin to rest. You begin to trust. And from that place of security flows a life of purpose, joy, and confidence in His plan.

**DEVOTIONAL THOUGHT**

### Wellness Habit

Write 3 biblical affirmations about your identity in Christ and declare them aloud today.

What are the lies you've believed about your worth?
What is God saying about who you truly are?

Reflection Prompt

**Prayer**
Father, remind me of who I am in You. Silence the lies that have shaped my thinking and help me walk in the truth that I am fearfully, wonderfully, and purposefully made. Amen.

## GRATITUDE & NOTES

Week 1: Day 3
# Walk in the Spirit
Spiritual Wholeness: Rooted In Christ

*"If the Spirit is the source of our life, we must also allow the Spirit to direct every aspect of our lives."*
Galatians 5:25 TPT

The Christian life was never meant to be powered by willpower. It's meant to be fueled by the Holy Spirit. This verse reminds us that walking in wholeness means walking in step with Him in our emotions, decisions, relationships, even our schedules.

Sometimes we compartmentalize our faith, inviting God into Sunday mornings or prayer times but forgetting He wants to guide us in all things even what we eat, how we speak, how we rest, and how we respond to stress.

When we walk in the Spirit, we begin to live in sync with Heaven. Peace replaces chaos. Grace replaces pressure. And every step becomes an act of surrender.

**DEVOTIONAL THOUGHT**

### Wellness Habit
Before each new task today, pause and whisper, "Holy Spirit, lead me here." Pay attention to how He responds.

Where in your life have you been leading yourself instead of letting the Spirit guide you?

Reflection Prompt

SPIRITUAL WHOLENESS: ROOTED IN CHRIST

**Prayer**: Holy Spirit, I invite You into the center of my life today. Teach me to walk with You in every thought and step. Help me surrender control and find peace in Your presence. Amen.

## GRATITUDE & NOTES

Week 1: Day 4
# Intimacy Over Perfection
Spiritual Wholeness: Rooted In Christ

*Surrender your anxiety. Be still and realize that I am God. I am God above all the nations, and I am exalted throughout the whole earth."*
Psalm 46:10 TPT

God desires your heart more than your hustle. So often we equate spiritual maturity with doing more, more Bible reading, more ministry, more good works. But God says: Be still. Not perform. Not prove. Simply know Him.

True intimacy grows in stillness. In the quiet space where you show up without an agenda just to be with your Father. This is where your soul exhales, your identity settles, and your spirit is refreshed.

Today, you are invited to step off the performance treadmill and rest in your belovedness. You don't have to earn what's already yours: God's attention, affection, and delight.

DEVOTIONAL THOUGHT

**Wellness Habit**
Spend 5 minutes today in stillness before God. No requests. No agenda. Just quiet listening.

What drives your spiritual activity intimacy with God, or fear of falling short?

Reflection Prompt

SPIRITUAL WHOLENESS: ROOTED IN CHRIST

**Prayer**

Father, forgive me for the times I've tried to perform for You instead of just being with You. Draw me back to intimacy. Help me slow down and hear Your voice again. I want to know You deeply not just serve You dutifully. Amen.

## GRATITUDE & NOTES

Week 1: Day 5
# Rooted in His Word
Spiritual Wholeness: Rooted In Christ

 *"Fill your thoughts with my words until they penetrate deep into your spirit."* Proverbs 4:21 TPT

The Word of God is not just information it's transformation. When we soak in Scripture, we're not just learning about God, we're being shaped by Him. His Word becomes the anchor for our emotions, decisions, and identity.

Too often we treat the Bible like a checkbox or a duty. But what if it was your lifeline? What if His words were the nourishment your heart craved?

Being rooted in the Word means more than reading a verse it means letting the truth take root in you. Today, let His word be more than ink on a page. Let it be breath to your bones.

DEVOTIONAL THOUGHT

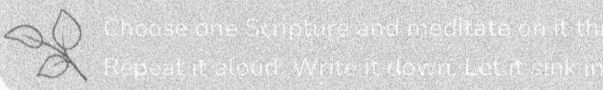

### Wellness Habit
Choose one Scripture and meditate on it throughout the day. Repeat it aloud. Write it down. Let it sink in.

What verse or passage is God highlighting to you today?

Reflection Prompt

SPIRITUAL WHOLENESS: ROOTED IN CHRIST

**Prayer**

God, I want to love Your Word again. Stir a hunger in me for truth. Let Your voice be the loudest one I hear. Plant Your promises deep in my heart so they shape the way I think, speak, and live. Amen.

## GRATITUDE & NOTES

Week 1: Day 6
# Return to Rest
Spiritual Wholeness: Rooted In Christ

 *"On that day, the root of Jesse will be lifted up as a miracle sign to rally the people. Gentiles will diligently seek Him, and His resting place will be glorious!"* Isaiah 11:10 TPT

Rest is not laziness it's warfare. In a culture of burnout, resting in God is an act of resistance. It declares I trust You, not my hustle. I rely on grace, not grind.

Many of us feel guilty when we rest. But God's rhythm for your wholeness includes rest. He built it into creation not as an afterthought, but as a gift. Jesus Himself often withdrew to lonely places to rest and pray. If the Savior needed it, so do we.

True rest restores. It reminds us that we are loved for who we are not what we do. Return to that place today.

**DEVOTIONAL THOUGHT**

 **Wellness Habit**
Block 30 minutes today for intentional rest. No screens. No work. Just be. Pray, journal, or nap guilt-free.

What's one area of your life where you need to return to rest?

 Reflection Prompt

**Prayer**

Jesus, You invite me into rest not just physically, but in my spirit. Teach me how to slow down and find my peace in You. Help me to resist the pressure to always be producing and help me to receive the grace to be. Amen

## GRATITUDE & NOTES

Week 1: Day 7
# Fully Known, Deeply Loved
Spiritual Wholeness: Rooted In Christ

*"You perceive every movement of my heart and soul, and You understand my every thought before it even enters my mind."* Psalm 139:2 TPT

You are fully seen and fully loved. God knows every thought, fear, and flaw and He doesn't flinch. In fact, His love runs toward you, not away. This is the kind of knowing that heals. The kind of love that transforms.

When you believe you are deeply loved, shame begins to fall off. You stop hiding. You stop performing. You begin to live freely, boldly, and wholly not to earn love, but because you already have it.

Today, let His perfect love silence every voice that says you're too much or not enough. Rest in the truth: you are already chosen, cherished, and seen.

**DEVOTIONAL THOUGHT**

### Wellness Habit
Look in the mirror today and speak this aloud: 'I am fully known and deeply loved by God.' Say it until you believe it.

What would your life look like if you truly believed God loved you fully and always?

SPIRITUAL WHOLENESS: ROOTED IN CHRIST

**Prayer**

Father, thank You for knowing me completely and still choosing me. Heal every place in me that doubts Your love. Help me to walk in the confidence of a beloved child. Let Your love be the foundation of my wholeness. Amen.

 **GRATITUDE & NOTES**

# Weekly Reflection & Gratitude Journal

**REFLECTIONS:**

Reflection invites us to see where God has been moving in our lives. As you pause at the end of the week, look back not with shame, but with grace. Celebrate what God has done, bring your struggles to Him, and write with honesty—knowing He meets you in every moment.

**GRATITUDE JOURNAL:**

Gratitude anchors our hearts in God's goodness—through both the calm and the chaos. Take a moment to list three things from this week that stirred thankfulness in your spirit. Maybe it was a quiet moment, a kind word, or simply God's nearness. Nothing is too small; every blessing is a gift from Him.

Week 2: Day 8
# Renew Your Mind
Mental Wholeness: Renewed in Truth

*"Stop imitating the ideals and opinions of the culture around you but be inwardly transformed by the Holy Spirit through a total reformation of how you think. This will empower you to discern God's will as you live a beautiful life, satisfying and perfect in His eyes.' Romans 12:2 TPT*

Your mind is the gateway to your transformation. What you think on, dwell in, and agree with shapes your reality. The Holy Spirit wants to rewire not just your behavior but your belief system.

The world will try to conform you into its mold through fear, anxiety, and lies. But God is inviting you into a renewed mind: a mind that sees through truth, thinks with clarity, and aligns with Heaven's perspective. Let today be the beginning of that renewal.

**DEVOTIONAL THOUGHT**

**Wellness Habit**
Write down 3 lies you've been believing and replace them with truth from Scripture.

What thoughts have you been believing that don't line up with God's truth?

Reflection Prompt

**Prayer**

Holy Spirit, transform my thinking. Help me identify and reject the lies I've believed. Renew my mind with Your truth and give me clarity, focus, and peace. Amen.

## GRATITUDE & NOTES

Week 2: Day 9
# Fix Your Thoughts
Mental Wholeness: Renewed in Truth

 *"Keep your thoughts continually fixed on all that is authentic and real, honorable and admirable, beautiful and respectful, pure and holy, merciful and kind. And fasten your thoughts on every glorious work of God, praising Him always"* Philippians 4:8 TPT

Your thought life is not neutral its formative. Paul gives us a filter: only let in what is worthy of praise. Not every thought deserves your attention. Some need to be cast down and replaced.

Mental wellness means becoming intentional about where your mind goes when it wanders. Fixing your thoughts on what is good creates space for joy, gratitude, and peace to flourish.

**DEVOTIONAL THOUGHT**

 **Wellness Habit**
Set a reminder to pause 3 times today and reflect on what you've been thinking about. Redirect your thoughts to something beautiful.

What do your daily thoughts sound like? Are they life giving or draining?

MENTAL WHOLENESS: RENEWED IN TRUTH

25

**Prayer**

Father, train my mind to focus on what is true and good. I surrender anxious and critical thoughts and ask for a renewed focus on Your goodness. Amen.

## GRATITUDE & NOTES

Week 2: Day 10

# Take Every Thought Captive

Mental Wholeness: Renewed in Truth

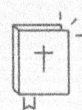

"'We can demolish every deceptive fantasy that opposes God and break through every arrogant attitude that is raised up in defiance of the true knowledge of God. We capture, like prisoners of war, every thought and insist that it bow in obedience to the Anointed One"   2 Corinthians 10:5 TPT

**DEVOTIONAL THOUGHT**

You don't have to believe everything you think. Some thoughts are intruders lies from the enemy meant to keep you bound in fear or shame. God gives you authority to take those thoughts captive and make them obey truth.

Mental wholeness isn't about having perfect thoughts it's about learning how to respond when unhealthy thoughts show up. Today is an invitation to take back mental ground.

**Wellness Habit**

When a negative or anxious thought hits today, pause and ask: "Is this true? Is this from God?" Then speak truth over it.

What thoughts are trying to take you captive right now?

MENTAL WHOLENESS: RENEWED IN TRUTH

**Prayer**

Jesus, help me take every thought captive. Give me discernment to recognize what doesn't belong, and strength to stand in Your truth. Amen.

## GRATITUDE & NOTES

Week 2: Day 11
# Set Your Mind On Things Above
Mental Wholeness: Renewed in Truth

*"Yes, feast on all the treasures of the Heavenly realm and fill your thoughts with Heavenly realities, and not with the distractions of the natural realm." Colossians 3:2 TPT*

**DEVOTIONAL THOUGHT**

Your mind is like a compass it points toward whatever you focus on most. Paul urges us to set our thoughts not on the noise of the world, but on the beauty of Heaven's reality. Mental renewal begins with intentional focus.

That doesn't mean we ignore life's challenges, but we choose what we center our attention on. Fixing your mind on God's truth doesn't just bring peace, it shifts your entire inner atmosphere.

Heaven's perspective brings clarity. It reminds you that you're seated with Christ, not stuck in chaos. Set your mind today like a thermostat — not reacting to every temperature but establishing it through truth.

### Wellness Habit
Write out Colossians 3:2 and place it somewhere visible today. When distraction hits, read it aloud and reset your focus.

What distractions or worries are occupying your thoughts most?
What does Heaven say about them?

Reflection Prompt

**Prayer**: Jesus, lift my eyes today. Help me to see with Heaven's clarity. I choose to fill my thoughts with truth, not fear with grace, not noise. Reset my mental atmosphere by Your Spirit. Amen.

## GRATITUDE & NOTES

Week 2: Day 12
# Guard Your Heart and Mind
Mental Wholeness: Renewed in Truth

*"Then God's wonderful peace that transcends human understanding, will guard your heart and mind through Jesus Christ."* Philippians 4:7 TPT

Peace is not passive. It's protective. When you stay rooted in prayer and gratitude, God's peace becomes a guard a shield for your emotions and your thoughts.

Many times, we try to guard ourselves through control, overthinking, or shutting down. But divine peace does the guarding far better than we can. It quiets fear, disarms anxiety, and invites you into holy stillness.

Instead of asking 'How can I fix this?' begin asking, 'God, how can I rest in You here?' His peace is not logical it's supernatural. Let it guard you today.

DEVOTIONAL THOUGHT

**Wellness Habit:**
Pause and take three deep breaths. Whisper, "Jesus, guard my heart and mind." Do this anytime you feel anxious today.

What would it look like for you to let peace guard your mind today instead of fear or control?

**Prayer**

God, I welcome Your peace to guard my heart and mind today. Not my fear, not my striving — but Your Spirit. Quiet the inner noise and help me rest in Your perfect care. Amen.

## GRATITUDE & NOTES

Week 2: Day 13
# Be Transformed by Renewal
Mental Wholeness: Renewed in Truth

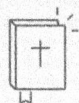

> *Stop imitating the ideals and opinions of the culture around you but be inwardly transformed by the Holy Spirit through a total reformation of how you think. This will empower you to discern God's will as you live a beautiful life, satisfying and perfect in His eyes."* Romans 12:2 TPT

You were made to stand out, not to blend in. Transformation happens when the Holy Spirit renews your thought patterns not with worldly ideas, but with Kingdom truth.

Culture may say, 'do more,' 'prove yourself,' or 'you're not enough.' But the Spirit gently reshapes our minds to align with Heaven: 'You are already loved.' 'You are chosen.' 'You are being renewed.'

Mental wellness starts with thinking differently and that begins by inviting the Holy Spirit to show you what to release, and what to believe.

**DEVOTIONAL THOUGHT**

**Wellness Habit**
Read Romans 12:2 aloud each morning this week. Declare: "I am not conformed; I am transformed by truth."

What cultural pressures are shaping your thoughts right now? What truth is the Holy Spirit inviting you to believe instead?

Reflection Prompt

**Prayer**

Holy Spirit, I give You full access to my thinking today. Transform me from the inside out. Help me think like Jesus, the King of Heaven and Earth, and to reflect His love in my mind, emotions, and habits. Amen

## GRATITUDE & NOTES

Week 2: Day 14
# A Sound Mind
Mental Wholeness: Renewed in Truth

*"For God will never give you the spirit of fear, but the Holy Spirit who gives you mighty power, love, and self-control."*
2 Timothy 1:7 TPT

Fear is not your inheritance peace is. Scripture calls it a 'sound mind,' a mind that is disciplined, stable, and full of love. This is what the Spirit gives, not anxiety or confusion.

So often, fear whispers louder than truth. But when you know what you've been given power, love, and self-control fear begins to lose its grip.

Speak it aloud today: 'God has given me a sound mind.' You don't have to figure it all out. Just return to the Spirit, and let Him fill you again.

**DEVOTIONAL THOUGHT**

**Wellness Habit**
Each time fear rises today, speak 2 Timothy 1:7 aloud and declare, 'I have a sound mind.'

Where has fear been louder than truth in your mind lately? What would shift if you embraced your sound mind?

Reflection Prompt

**Prayer** — Lord, I thank You that fear is not from You. Today, I receive the Spirit of power, love, and self-control. I walk in the truth that I am grounded, clear, and held by You. Amen.

## GRATITUDE & NOTES

# Weekly Reflection & Gratitude Journal

**REFLECTIONS:**

Reflection invites us to see where God has been moving in our lives. As you pause at the end of the week, look back not with shame, but with grace. Celebrate what God has done, bring your struggles to Him, and write with honesty—knowing He meets you in every moment.

**GRATITUDE JOURNAL:**

Gratitude anchors our hearts in God's goodness through both the calm and the chaos. Take a moment to list three things from this week that stirred thankfulness in your spirit. Maybe it was a quiet moment, a kind word, or simply God's nearness. Nothing is too small; every blessing is a gift from Him.

Week 3: Day 15
# Your Body is His Temple
Physical Wholeness: Honouring the Body

 *"Have you forgotten that your body is now the sacred temple of the Spirit of Holiness, who lives in you? You don't belong to yourself any longer, for the gift of God, the Holy Spirit, lives inside your sanctuary"* 1 Corinthians 6:19 TPT

You were not given your body to be at war with it. Scripture reminds us that your body is not a burden it's a temple. A dwelling place for God's Spirit.

This means your body is sacred. It is worthy of care, respect, and gratitude. When we honor our physical health, we're not indulging the flesh we're worshipping the Creator who formed it.

Let this truth settle in: your body is not a project to perfect but a vessel to steward. Today, start from love not shame.

**DEVOTIONAL THOUGHT**

### Wellness Habit
 Stand in front of a mirror and thank God for 3 things about your physical body — its strength, beauty, or function.

In what ways have you seen your body as less than sacred? How can you begin to shift that mindset?

Reflection Prompt

**Prayer** — Holy Spirit, I welcome You into every part of my body. Help me honor this temple, not with pressure but with peace. Teach me to care for it with grace and love. Amen.

## GRATITUDE & NOTES

Week 3: Day 16
# Strength in Surrender
Physical Wholeness: Honouring the Body

 *So, I'm not defeated by my weakness but delighted! For when I feel my weakness and endure mistreatment, when I'm surrounded with troubles on every side and face persecution because of my love for Christ, I am made yet stronger. For my weakness becomes a portal to God's power.*
2 Corinthians 12:10 TPT

Physical wholeness isn't about perfection it's about surrender. When you are tired, weak, or facing health limitations, you're not disqualified. In fact, you're in the perfect place to encounter Christ's strength.

Instead of pushing through burnout, pause. Let His power be your source. Your body was never meant to be your god Jesus is. And He meets you in your weakness with compassion and strength.

**DEVOTIONAL THOUGHT**

**Wellness Habit**
Slow down. Choose one way to physically rest or nourish yourself today guilt-free.

Where do you feel weak or tired in your body today? What would it look like to invite Jesus into that space?

**Prayer**

Jesus, thank You for meeting me in weakness. Help me not to hide or hustle, but to rest in Your strength. I surrender my body to You. Amen.

## GRATITUDE & NOTES

Week 3: Day 17
# Rest is Holy
Physical Wholeness: Honouring the Body

 *"Are you weary, carrying a heavy burden? Come to me. I will refresh your life, for I am your oasis"* Matt 11:28 TPT

Rest is not a reward it's a rhythm of wholeness. God created rest before humanity ever worked. That means you are not defined by how much you do, but by Who you dwell with.

True physical wholeness includes honoring the need to pause. To breathe. To stop striving. When you rest, you reflect the heart of the Creator who rested, too.

Rest is holy ground — not laziness, but worship. Today, let go of guilt and receive it as sacred.

**DEVOTIONAL THOUGHT**

 **Wellness Habit**
Schedule 20 minutes of intentional rest today: a nap, a slow walk, or simply breathing deeply in silence.

How do you typically feel about rest? Is it hard to slow down? Why?

**Prayer**

Father, teach me to rest. Help me see it not as a weakness, but as worship. I receive the holiness of stillness today. Amen.

## GRATITUDE & NOTES

Week 3: Day 18

# Nourish, Don't Punish
Physical Wholeness: Honouring the Body

 *"So, whether you eat or drink, live your life in a way that glorifies and honors God."* 1 Corinthians 10:31 TPT

God cares about what you eat not out of control, but care. Eating is not just physical; it's spiritual. You were never meant to punish your body with restriction or shame.

Nourishment is about alignment. What honors your body? What fuels peace, strength, and clarity? Invite the Holy Spirit into your plate, and let food become an act of worship, not worry.

**DEVOTIONAL THOUGHT**

### Wellness Habit
Choose one meal today to eat slowly, with gratitude. Pray before and after, inviting God into the experience.

How have you viewed food as a gift or as a struggle? What mindset shift is God inviting you into?

PHYSICAL WHOLENESS: HONOURING THE BODY

**Prayer**

God, thank You for the gift of food. Teach me to nourish my body with love and wisdom. Let my habits reflect Your grace, not guilt. Amen.

## GRATITUDE & NOTES

Week 3: Day 19
# Movement as Worship
Physical Wholeness: Honouring the Body

 *Put your heart and soul into every activity you do, as though you are doing it for the Lord Himself and not merely for others"* Colossians 3:23 TPT

Your body was made to move not as punishment, but as praise. Movement is not about changing how you look. It's about honoring what God gave you.

When you walk, stretch, dance, or breathe deeply, you're partnering with the design He created. Let your movement be joy-filled, Spirit-led, and free of comparison. It's worship in motion.

**DEVOTIONAL THOUGHT**

 **Wellness Habit**
Move your body today in a way that feels worshipful: a walk, dancing to worship music, stretching, etc.

What forms of movement bring you joy and connection? How can you approach them with freedom, not pressure?

**Prayer:** Lord, thank You for my body. I choose to move today not to earn worth, but to express gratitude. Let every step be worship. Amen.

## GRATITUDE & NOTES

Week 3: Day 20
# Your Body is a Gift
Physical Wholeness: Honouring the Body

 *"I thank you, God, for making me so mysteriously complex! Everything you do is marvelously breathtaking. It simply amazes me to think about it! How thoroughly you know me, Lord"* Psalm 139:14 TPT

You are not random. You are a masterpiece. That includes your physical body its features, its limits, its strengths. Your body is a gift, not a problem to fix.

Comparison steals gratitude. But celebration restores wholeness. What would shift if you truly believed your body was worthy of love right now, as it is?

**DEVOTIONAL THOUGHT**

### Wellness Habit
Look in the mirror and speak Psalm 139:14 over yourself. Say it until it settles as truth.

What have you criticized about your body that God may be inviting you to celebrate?

Reflection Prompt

**Prayer:** Father, forgive me for seeing my body through the lens of criticism. I receive Your declaration that I am wonderfully made. Help me live in celebration. Amen.

## GRATITUDE & NOTES

Week 3: Day 21
# Wholeness is Worship
Physical Wholeness: Honouring the Body

 " *Beloved friends, what should be our proper response to God's marvelous mercies? To surrender yourselves to God to be His sacred, living sacrifices. And live in holiness, experiencing all that delights His heart. For this becomes your genuine expression of worship.*"
Romans 12:1 TPT

This is the heart of physical wholeness: surrender. When we offer our bodies not just our minds or spirits as worship, everything shifts.

Your wellness is not about image. It's about intimacy. It's about choosing to let every breath, every habit, every moment reflect His glory. You are a living act of worship.

*DEVOTIONAL THOUGHT*

**Wellness Habit**
Write a short letter to God, offering your body to Him again as a vessel of worship, not performance.

What does it mean to surrender your physical health to God?
What step could you take toward that today?

*Reflection Prompt*

PHYSICAL WHOLENESS: HONOURING THE BODY

**Prayer**

Jesus, my whole life is Yours, body, mind, and spirit. I surrender my physical habits to You and choose to live as a sacred offering. Amen.

## GRATITUDE & NOTES

*PHYSICAL WHOLENESS: HONOURING THE BODY*

# Weekly Reflection & Gratitude Journal

REFLECTIONS:

Reflection invites us to see where God has been moving in our lives. As you pause at the end of the week, look back not with shame, but with grace. Celebrate what God has done, bring your struggles to Him, and write with honesty knowing He meets you in every moment.

GRATITUDE JOURNAL:

Gratitude anchors our hearts in God's goodness through both the calm and the chaos. Take a moment to list three things from this week that stirred thankfulness in your spirit. Maybe it was a quiet moment, a kind word, or simply God's nearness. Nothing is too small; every blessing is a gift from Him.

Week 4: Day 22
# Emotions are not the Enemy
Emotional Wholeness: Feeling Fully, Healing Deeply

 *"Pour out all your worries and stress upon Him and leave them there, for He always tenderly cares for you."*
1 Peter 5:7 TPT

Emotions are not a sign of weakness they're a part of your design. God doesn't ask us to suppress them; He invites us to bring them to Him.

Often, we try to manage, hide, or even shame our feelings. But the Psalms show us that God is not afraid of raw emotion. He welcomes your honesty. Healing begins not when you 'get over it,' but when you bring your heart fully to Him.

Let today be a release not a retreat. Pour it all out before the One who truly cares.

**DEVOTIONAL THOUGHT**

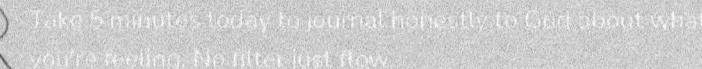

**Wellness Habit**
Take 5 minutes today to journal honestly to God about what you're feeling. No filter, just flow.

What emotions have you been carrying alone? How can you pour them out to God today?

**Prayer**

Lord, I bring my emotions to You today. The messy ones, the silent ones, the loud ones. Thank You that I don't have to hide. Meet me in them and bring healing. Amen.

## GRATITUDE & NOTES

Week 4: Day 23
# Jesus Wept
Emotional Wholeness: Feeling Fully, Healing Deeply

 *"Then tears streamed down Jesus' face."* John 11:35 TPT

This is the shortest verse in the Bible and one of the most powerful. Jesus knew He was about to raise Lazarus, yet He still wept. He entered the pain of the moment. He felt it, honored it, and didn't rush past it.

God doesn't demand you 'get over it' quickly. Your tears are not a problem they are sacred. If Jesus wept, you are allowed to, too.

Let His compassion meet you in your sorrow. He is with you not just in the breakthrough, but in the breakdown.

DEVOTIONAL THOUGHT

**Wellness Habit**
Light a candle or sit in silence today for 5 minutes and simply let yourself "feel". You are safe to do so.

What grief or sorrow are you carrying? What would it look like to invite Jesus to sit with you in it?

Reflection Prompt

**Prayer**

Jesus, thank You that You weep with me. You understand my pain, and You don't rush me through it. Help me feel fully so I can heal deeply. Amen.

## GRATITUDE & NOTES

Week 4: Day 24
# Joy Comes in the Morning
Emotional Wholeness: Feeling Fully, Healing Deeply

*"I've learned that His anger lasts for a moment, but His loving favor lasts a lifetime! We may weep through the night, but at daybreak it will turn into shouts of ecstatic joy"*
Psalm 30:5 TPT

Emotional wholeness embraces the full range of feeling sorrow and joy, lament and praise. This verse reminds us that pain is not permanent. God is not finished in the dark. Morning always comes.

This doesn't mean we fake joy. It means we hold onto hope. Joy is coming. It may start as a whisper before it's a shout but it's coming.

Trust that God is working through your night seasons. His joy is deeper than your circumstance and it's already breaking in.

DEVOTIONAL THOUGHT

**Wellness Habit**
Write down 3 things that give you hope today, no matter how small. Let them anchor your heart.

Where in your life are you still waiting for joy to rise? What hope can you hold onto in the meantime?

Reflection Prompt

**Prayer**

God, thank You that joy comes again. Even in the nights of my soul, You are working. Help me hold onto hope and trust Your light will rise. Amen.

## GRATITUDE & NOTES

Week 4: Day 25
# Peace in the Storm
Emotional Wholeness: Feeling Fully, Healing Deeply

*"That evening, the disciples gathered together, and because they were afraid of reprisals from the Jewish leaders, they had locked the doors. But suddenly Jesus appeared among them and said, "Peace to you!"  John 20:19 TPT*

**DEVOTIONAL THOUGHT**

Jesus speaks peace not only before the storm, but in the middle of it. When the disciples were full of fear, hiding behind locked doors, Jesus showed up and brought peace.

He doesn't wait for you to 'calm down' before He enters in. He meets you right where your emotions are unsettled and He speaks peace that surpasses logic.

Even if your circumstances haven't changed, His presence can change your heart. Let Him speak 'Peace to you' today.

### Wellness Habit
Each time you feel overwhelmed today, take a deep breath and whisper, 'Jesus, I receive Your peace.'

What emotional storm have you been navigating lately? What would it look like to let Jesus speak peace into it?

Reflection Prompt

**Prayer**

Jesus, You are my peace. Even in my emotional storms, You meet me with calm. Help me let go of fear and anchor myself in Your presence. Amen

## GRATITUDE & NOTES

Week 4: Day 26
# Freedom from Shame
Emotional Wholeness: Feeling Fully, Healing Deeply

 *"So now every righteous requirement of the law can be fulfilled through the Anointed One living His life in us. And we are free to live, not according to our flesh, but by the dynamic power of the Holy Spirit!"* Romans 8:4 TPT

Shame is a heavy weight and it's not from God. While conviction leads to healing, shame leads to hiding. But the Holy Spirit doesn't shame you, He frees you.

Whatever you're carrying emotionally, bring it into the light. Shame grows in silence but dies in truth. You are not what you feel or what you've done, you are who God says you are.

Let today be a declaration: shame no longer has a voice in your life. You are free.

**DEVOTIONAL THOUGHT**

### Wellness Habit
Write out Romans 8:4 and declare it aloud today. Let truth interrupt shame's narrative.

What emotional weight have you been carrying in secret? What truth can you speak to silence shame?

**Prayer** Holy Spirit, thank You for setting me free from shame. Help me live in the light and speak truth over my emotions. I receive freedom today. Amen.

 **GRATITUDE & NOTES**

Week 4: Day 27
# Speak to Your Soul
Emotional Wholeness: Feeling Fully, Healing Deeply

*"So I say to my soul, 'Don't be discouraged. Don't be disturbed. For I know my God will break through for me' Then I'll have plenty of reasons to praise Him all over again. Yes, He is my saving grace!"* Psalm 42:11 TPT

**DEVOTIONAL THOUGHT**

Sometimes your soul needs a reminder. David didn't wait until he *felt* better he spoke truth to his own soul.

Your emotions may not always align with truth, but you have the authority to guide them. Not with harshness, but with hope. Speaking to your soul isn't denial it's discipleship.

Today, talk to your soul with kindness and faith. Remind it who your God is.

**Wellness Habit**
Write a short letter or affirmation to your soul today. Beginning with "Dear soul..."

What does your soul need to hear today? How can you lovingly speak truth to it?

Reflection Prompt

**Prayer** Father, teach me to speak to my soul with truth and gentleness. Thank You that I can partner with You in leading my emotions into peace. Amen.

## GRATITUDE & NOTES

Week 4: Day 28
# Wholehearted Living
Emotional Wholeness: Feeling Fully, Healing Deeply

 *"So above all, guard the affections of your heart, for they affect all that you are. Pay attention to the welfare of your innermost being, for from there flows the wellspring of life"* Proverbs 4:23 TPT

Emotional wholeness isn't about perfection. It's about living with your whole heart open, surrendered, and guarded by truth.

When you guard your heart, you protect the wellspring of your life. Not with walls, but with wisdom. The goal isn't to stop feeling it's to feel with God.

Invite Him to help you live wholeheartedly today anchored in grace, not ruled by emotion.

**DEVOTIONAL THOUGHT**

**Wellness Habit**
Set a 10-minute boundary today for emotional self-care no phone, no pressure, just stillness and God

Where do you feel emotionally drained? What would it mean to guard your heart without shutting it down?

**Prayer** God, I give You my heart the full range of it. Teach me to guard it with wisdom and live wholeheartedly in Your presence. Amen.

## GRATITUDE & NOTES

# Weekly Reflection & Gratitude Journal

REFLECTIONS:

Reflection invites us to see where God has been moving in our lives. As you pause at the end of the week, look back not with shame, but with grace. Celebrate what God has done, bring your struggles to Him, and write with honesty knowing He meets you in every moment.

GRATITUDE JOURNAL:

Gratitude anchors our hearts in God's goodness through both the calm and the chaos. Take a moment to list three things from this week that stirred thankfulness in your spirit. Maybe it was a quiet moment, a kind word, or simply God's nearness. Nothing is too small; every blessing is a gift from Him.

Week 5: Day 29
# Loved to Love
Relational Wholeness: Cultivating Christlike Connection

 *"I give you now a new commandment: Love each other just as much as I have loved you."* John 13:34 TPT

Love flows from being loved. Jesus didn't ask us to manufacture love He modeled it. When we receive His deep, personal, faithful love, it fills us up and spills out to others.

Your ability to love others well begins with how rooted you are in God's love for *you*. You don't have to strive or stretch beyond your capacity. You simply stay close to the Source.

Let today be about receiving first so you can give without running dry.

**Wellness Habit**
Spend 5 minutes in stillness simply repeating, "I am deeply loved by God." Let it sink in.

How has your relationship with God shaped how you relate to others?

**Prayer:** Jesus, thank You for loving me first. Help me love others the way You love me fully, freely, and without fear. Amen.

## GRATITUDE & NOTES

Week 5: Day 30
# Boundaries are Biblical
Relational Wholeness: Cultivating Christlike Connection

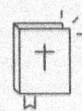

*"But I have this complaint against you. You are permitting that woman that Jezebel who calls herself a prophet to lead my servants astray. She teaches them to commit sexual sin and to eat food offered to idols." Revelation 2:20 NLT*

Jesus was full of compassion but He also had boundaries. He walked away from toxic crowds, rested when tired, and didn't say yes to every demand.

Boundaries are not walls to keep people out, but gates to keep your heart safe and whole. They honor God, your limits, and others.

Today, reflect on where you need permission to say 'no' and trust that God blesses wisdom, not people-pleasing.

**DEVOTIONAL THOUGHT**

### Wellness Habit
Practice saying 'no' to something small today with love and clarity. Watch how peace follows.

Where do you need to set or reinforce a boundary in your life?

**Prayer:** God, give me wisdom and courage to set healthy boundaries. Help me protect what You've entrusted to me including my peace. Amen.

## GRATITUDE & NOTES

Week 5: Day 31
# Forgiveness Frees You
Relational Wholeness: Cultivating Christlike Connection

 *And when you pray, make sure you forgive the faults of others so that your Father in Heaven will also forgive you"* Matthew 6:14 TPT

Forgiveness isn't forgetting. It's choosing freedom. When we withhold forgiveness, we chain ourselves to past pain. But when we forgive, we release ourselves into peace.

Forgiveness doesn't mean trust or reconciliation it means surrender. Giving the offense to God. Letting Him be the healer and the judge.

Who are you carrying in your heart today? Can you begin to release them, one small step at a time?

**DEVOTIONAL THOUGHT**

### Wellness Habit
Pray a simple blessing over the person you're forgiving today. Whisper it even if it's hard.

Who do you need to forgive not for their sake, but for yours? What's one step you can take today?

**Prayer:** Lord, I choose to forgive. Help my heart follow where my faith leads. Set me free from bitterness. I trust You with the outcome. Amen.

 **GRATITUDE & NOTES**

Week 5: Day 32
# Conflict Can Be Holy
Relational Wholeness: Cultivating Christlike Connection

 *"But instead be kind and affectionate toward one another. Has God graciously forgiven you? Then graciously forgive one another in the depths of Christ's love."* Ephesians 4:32 TPT

Conflict is not always a sign of failure sometimes it's a door to deeper connection. When handled with grace, truth, and love, it can lead to growth.

God isn't afraid of your disagreements. He just wants you to walk through them with humility and mercy. Speak truth in love, listen to understand, and let peace guide your heart.

Holiness isn't avoiding conflict it's entering it like Jesus would.

DEVOTIONAL THOUGHT

**Wellness Habit**
Initiate one healing conversation this week. Ask God to lead it with gentleness and wisdom.

Is there a relationship where you're avoiding a hard conversation?
What might grace and truth look like there?

Reflection Prompt

**Prayer**

Holy Spirit, give me patience and kindness in conflict. Help me value connection over control. Let me reflect Your heart in hard places. Amen.

## GRATITUDE & NOTES

Week 5: Day 33
# Chosen Family
Relational Wholeness: Cultivating Christlike Connection

*"But you are God's chosen treasure, priests who are kings, a spiritual "nation" set apart as God's devoted ones. He called you out of darkness to experience His marvelous light, and now He claims you as His very own. He did this so that you would broadcast His glorious wonders throughout the world."* 1 Peter 2:9 TPT

Sometimes the most sacred relationships aren't biological — they're spiritual. God places people in your life who walk with you, pray with you, and lift you up.

You are part of God's chosen family, and you also have the power to create community rooted in Him. Don't wait for perfect people. Build with the willing.

Today, thank God for the spiritual siblings, mentors, and friends who help you become whole.

**DEVOTIONAL THOUGHT**

**Wellness Habit**
Send a message of encouragement or gratitude to someone who's been part of your spiritual journey.

Who has been a spiritual family member in your life?
How can you honour or bless them today?

Reflection Prompt

**Prayer**

God, thank You for placing people in my life who reflect Your love. Help me be that kind of person for others, too. Amen.

## GRATITUDE & NOTES

Week 5: Day 34
# Let Love Lead
## Relational Wholeness: Cultivating Christlike Connection

"Let love be your highest goal! But you should also desire the special abilities the Spirit gives especially the ability to prophesy." 1 Corinthians 14:1 NLT

It's easy to lead with fear, control, or self-protection but God invites you to let love lead. Love may not always feel safe, but it's always powerful.

When love leads, you listen longer, forgive quicker, and stay anchored in grace. Not because people are perfect, but because Jesus is.

Let today be an invitation to make love your default response, not just your ideal.

**DEVOTIONAL THOUGHT**

**Wellness Habit**
Before speaking today, pause and ask, "Is what I'm about to say rooted in love?"

What relationship or interaction today needs to be led by love rather than reaction?

**Prayer**: Jesus, help me lead with love in my words, actions, and intentions. Let Your love shape every part of how I relate to others. Amen.

## GRATITUDE & NOTES

Week 5: Day 35
# Community Heals
Relational Wholeness: Cultivating Christlike Connection

 *"Love empowers us to fulfill the law of the Anointed One as we carry each other's troubles."* Galatians 6:2 TPT

## DEVOTIONAL THOUGHT

God never meant for you to do life alone. Healing often happens in the presence of safe people. Community is not just comfort it's medicine.

Wholeness grows when you let others carry part of your burden. That takes vulnerability, trust, and humility. But the reward is deep connection and mutual healing.

Let yourself be seen, supported, and surrounded today. You were made for community.

### Wellness Habit
Reach out to someone today and let them know how you're really doing. Let yourself be known.

What's one way you can show up more fully in community or let others show up for you?

**Prayer** — God, thank You for community. Teach me to open my heart, share my life, and carry others in love. I receive the healing that comes from connection. Amen.

## GRATITUDE & NOTES

# Weekly Reflection & Gratitude Journal

**REFLECTIONS:**

Reflection invites us to see where God has been moving in our lives. As you pause at the end of the week, look back not with shame, but with grace. Celebrate what God has done, bring your struggles to Him, and write with honesty knowing He meets you in every moment.

**GRATITUDE JOURNAL:**

Gratitude anchors our hearts in God's goodness through both the calm and the chaos. Take a moment to list three things from this week that stirred thankfulness in your spirit. Maybe it was a quiet moment, a kind word, or simply God's nearness. Nothing is too small; every blessing is a gift from Him.

Week 6: Day 36
# God is Your Provider
Financial Wholeness: Trusting God with our Treasures

"Consider the birds do you think they worry about their existence? They don't plant or reap or store up food, yet your Heavenly Father provides them each with food. Aren't you much more valuable to your Father than they?"
Matthew 6:26 TPT

Financial wholeness starts with this truth: God is your Provider. Not your job, not your bank account Him.

When Jesus pointed to the birds, He wasn't just talking about nature. He was speaking to your anxious thoughts. If God takes care of sparrows, He will certainly take care of you.

Let today be a shift from striving to trusting. He knows what you need and He's already making a way.

DEVOTIONAL THOUGHT

### Wellness Habit
Every time a worry about money comes up, say aloud: "God is my Provider."

Where do you feel anxious about moey? How can you surrender that anxiety to God today?

Reflection Prompt

**Prayer**

Father, I trust You. Even when things feel uncertain, I believe You care for me. Provide in Your perfect timing. Amen.

## GRATITUDE & NOTES

Week 6: Day 37
# Steward, Not Owner
Financial Wholeness: Trusting God with our Treasures

*Yahweh claims the world as His. Everything and everyone belong to Him!* Psalm 24:1 TPT

You are not the owner of what you have you're a steward. That truth lifts pressure and invites purpose.

When you manage what belongs to God, every dollar, decision, and desire becomes an opportunity to honor Him. It's not about perfection, it's about partnership.

Let stewardship shift how you view money not as a measure of success, but as a sacred trust.

**DEVOTIONAL THOUGHT**

### Wellness Habit
Take 10 minutes today to review where your money flows. Ask: Is this stewarding God's provision well?

What area of your finances do you need to realign with God's purpose?

 **Prayer** God, all I have is Yours. Help me be faithful with what You've given me. Show me how to steward it with wisdom. Amen.

 **GRATITUDE & NOTES**

Week 6: Day 38
# Break the Spirit of Lack
Financial Wholeness: Trusting God with our Treasures

*"Then He had everyone sit down on the grass and He then took the five loaves and two fish. He looked up into heaven, gave thanks to God, and broke the bread into pieces. He then gave it to his disciples, who in turn gave it to the crowds. And everyone ate until they were satisfied, for the food was multiplied in front of their eyes! They picked up the leftovers and filled up twelve baskets full!"* Matthew 14:19-20 TPT

The spirit of lack says, "It's not enough." But Jesus takes what looks small and multiplies it.

Gratitude is the first step to breaking lack. When Jesus gave thanks for the little, it became more than enough. Financial wholeness doesn't begin with increase it begins with perspective.

Speak gratitude today over what you do have and watch how God multiplies peace and provision.

**DEVOTIONAL THOUGHT**

**Wellness Habit**
Write a gratitude list of 5 financial blessings big or small. Give thanks for each.

Where have you been focused on what you don't have? What can you give thanks for instead?

Reflection Prompt

**Prayer**

Jesus, I choose to see abundance, not lack. Thank You for what I have. I trust You to multiply it as You see fit. Amen.

## GRATITUDE & NOTES

Week 6: Day 39
# Contentment is Wealth
Financial Wholeness: Trusting God with our Treasures

*"Yet true godliness with contentment is itself great wealth"*
1 Timothy 6:6 NLT

The world says, 'More is better.' But God says, 'Contentment is better.'

Contentment isn't complacency it's confidence in God's sufficiency. It's peace that doesn't depend on possessions. When you live grateful and grounded, you're already rich.

Let today be a pause a holy sigh of relief knowing that with God, you have enough.

**DEVOTIONAL THOUGHT**

### Wellness Habit
Unplug from social media or ads for 1 hour today. Let your soul rest from comparison.

What would change in your heart if you believed you truly had enough?

Reflection Prompt

**Prayer:** Lord, teach me the beauty of contentment. I want to find joy in what I have, not strive after what I don't. Amen.

## GRATITUDE & NOTES

Week 6: Day 40
# Generosity Flows from Grace
Financial Wholeness: Trusting God with our Treasures

 *"Here's my point. A stingy sower will reap a meager harvest, but the one who sows from a generous spirit will reap an abundant harvest." 2 Corinthians 9:6 TPT*

Generosity isn't about how much you have it's about how freely you give. It's not a pressure; it's a privilege.

When grace flows in, generosity flows out. It's not always money it can be time, kindness, help, or encouragement. As you give, you mirror your generous God.

Ask Him who you can bless today and give as led, not out of guilt, but out of love.

**DEVOTIONAL THOUGHT**

### Wellness Habit
Give something away today money, time, a meal, a compliment and let it go joyfully.

What small way can you practice generosity today even if you feel stretched?

Reflection Prompt

**Prayer** God, You are generous with me. Help me reflect that generosity with joy and freedom. Amen.

## GRATITUDE & NOTES

Week 6: Day 41
# Money Doesn't Define You
Financial Wholeness: Trusting God with our Treasures

*"Don't keep hoarding for yourselves earthly treasures that can be stolen by thieves. Material wealth eventually rusts, decays, and loses its value. Instead, stockpile heavenly treasures for yourselves that cannot be stolen and will never rust, decay, or lose their value. For your heart will always pursue what you esteem as your treasure."* Matthew 6:19–21 TPT

Your worth is not your wage. Your value isn't in what you earn or own it's in who you are to God.

Financial wholeness includes healing from lies that tie identity to income. You are already loved, chosen, and worthy. Money is a tool, not a title.

Let today be a return to truth you are priceless, with or without a paycheck..

**DEVOTIONAL THOUGHT**

**Wellness Habit**
Write an 'I am' statement: I am not my balance. I am _____ in Christ.

Have you ever tied your identity to your financial situation? What does God say instead?

Reflection Prompt

**Prayer** — Father, help me see myself through Your eyes. Detach my identity from numbers and root it in truth. Amen.

## GRATITUDE & NOTES

Week 6: Day 42
# Trust for the Future
Financial Wholeness: Trusting God with our Treasures

 *"Trust in the Lord completely, and do not rely on your own opinions. With all your Heart rely on Him to guide you, and He will lead you in every decision you make. Become intimate with Him in whatever you do, and He will lead you wherever you go". Proverbs 3:5–6 (TPT)*

The future can feel uncertain but your trust isn't in the market or economy. It's in the God who holds time.

You may not know what's next, but you can know the One who leads you. Financial wholeness is ultimately about surrender. Rest in knowing that God is already in your tomorrow.

You can move forward in peace, not fear.

**DEVOTIONAL THOUGHT**

**Wellness Habit**

Write a short prayer letter to God about your financial future. Let it be honest and hopeful.

What future financial concern do you need to entrust to God today?

**Prayer** — *Lord, I surrender tomorrow to You. Lead me step by step. Provide what I need and grow my faith as I follow. Amen.*

## GRATITUDE & NOTES

# Weekly Reflection & Gratitude Journal

REFLECTIONS:

Reflection invites us to see where God has been moving in our lives. As you pause at the end of the week, look back not with shame, but with grace. Celebrate what God has done, bring your struggles to Him, and write with honesty knowing He meets you in every moment.

GRATITUDE JOURNAL:

Gratitude anchors our hearts in God's goodness through both the calm and the chaos. Take a moment to list three things from this week that stirred thankfulness in your spirit. Maybe it was a quiet moment, a kind word, or simply God's nearness. Nothing is too small; every blessing is a gift from Him.

# SELF-CARE CHECKLIST

*Self-care isn't an act but a loving commitment to oneself.
How did you cherish yourself this week?*

- [ ] Take a long bath
- [ ] Read for pleasure
- [ ] Go for a slow walk
- [ ] Read Biblical affirmations
- [ ] Journal your thoughts
- [ ] Try gentle stretching
- [ ] Cook a nourishing meal
- [ ] Mediate on a Scripture
- [ ] Gardening
- [ ] Paint or draw
- [ ] Engage in a hobby
- [ ] Listen to your favorite music
- [ ] Spend time with a loved one
- [ ] Watch a light-hearted movie
- [ ] Pamper yourself
- [ ] Take a short nap
- [ ] Go for a swim
- [ ] Practice gratitude
- [ ] Attend a workshop or class
- [ ] Explore a new place

# You are Rooted in Wholeness
## A Final Word to Bless You on the Journey Ahead

Beloved, you've completed a sacred journey not toward perfection, but toward wholeness.

You've explored your spirit, mind, body, emotions, relationships, and finances through the lens of God's heart for you. You've let Scripture shape your steps, prayer guide your heart, and reflection lead you deeper into His presence.

This journal may be complete, but your transformation continues.

Remember this: Wholeness is not a destination it's a rhythm of surrender and renewal.

Every time you choose rest over striving, prayer over pressure, or love over fear you're walking in wellness, in step with the Spirit.

🪴 You are planted in Christ.
🌱 You are nourished by truth.
🌸 You are growing in grace.
🍇 You are bearing fruit that lasts.

## Final Scripture

"Since we first heard about you, we've kept you always in our prayers that you would receive the perfect knowledge of God's pleasure over your lives, making you reservoirs of every kind of wisdom and spiritual understanding. We pray that you would walk in the ways of true righteousness, pleasing God in every good thing you do. Then you'll become fruit-bearing branches, yielding to his life, and maturing in the rich experience of knowing God in his fullness! And we pray that you would be energized with all his explosive power from the realm of his magnificent glory, filling you with great hope. Your hearts can soar with joyful gratitude when you think of how God made you worthy to receive the glorious inheritance freely given to us by living in the light".
Colossians 1:9-12 TPT

## Final Blessing

May you walk in freedom.
May you rest in grace.
May you trust in God's provision, purpose, and peace.
And may your wholeness be a light to others.

## Final Reflection

What has God done in you through these 6 weeks?
What rhythms of wholeness do you want to carry forward?

*Teya Gibson*

www.ingramcontent.com/pod-product-compliance
Lightning Source LLC
Chambersburg PA
CBHW061210070526
44583CB00025B/3192